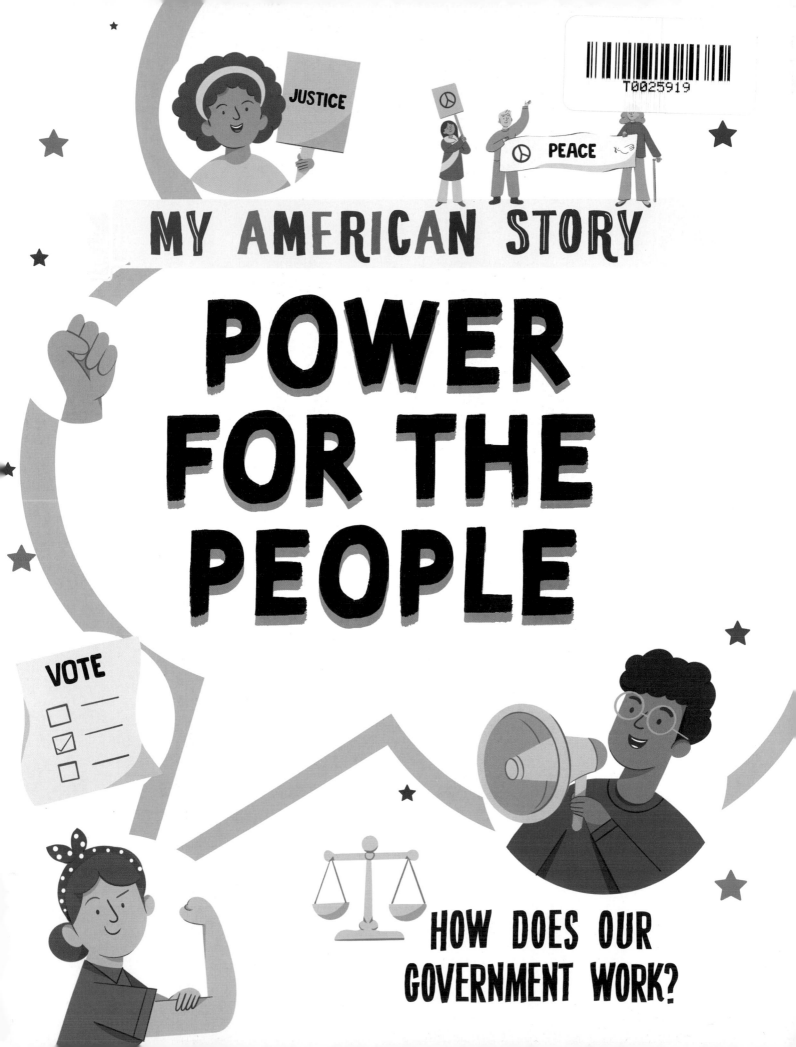

JUSTICE

PEACE

MY AMERICAN STORY

POWER FOR THE PEOPLE

VOTE

HOW DOES OUR GOVERNMENT WORK?

DK | Penguin Random House

Editorial Management by Oriel Square
Produced for DK by Collaborate Agency
Index by James Helling

Author Michael Burgan
Series Editor Megan DuVarney Forbes
Publisher Nick Hunter
Publisher Sarah Forbes
Publishing Project Manager Katherine Neep
Production Controller Isabell Schart
Picture Researcher Nunhoih Guite
Production Editor Shanker Prasad

First American Edition, 2023
Published in the United States by DK Publishing
1745 Broadway, 20th Floor, New York, NY 10019

The publisher would like to thank the following for their kind permission to reproduce their images:
(Key: a-above; b-below/bottom; c-center; f-far; l-left; r-right; t-top)

4 Getty Images: Hill Street Studios / DigitalVision (cl). **5 Getty Images:** Travelpix Ltd / Stone (tr). **6 Alamy Stock Photo**: IanDagnall Computing (cla). **Dreamstime.com:** Onur Ersin (br). **7 Alamy Stock Photo:** WDC Photos (c). **9 Library of Congress, Washington, D.C.:** U. S. Constitution. A bill of rights as provided in the ten original amendments to the constitution of the United States in force . n. p. 195. 1950. Pdf. https://www.loc.gov/item/rbpe.24404400/. (b). **10 Library of Congress, Washington, D.C.:** LC-DIG-pga-02797 / Strobridge & Co. Lith. (clb). **11 Alamy Stock Photo:** Photo Researchers / Science History Images (bl). Getty Images: Bettmann (cra). **12 Getty Images:** Chip Somodevilla / Staff (clb). **13 Library of Congress, Washington, D.C.:** LC-DIG-highsm-12576 / Highsmith, Carol M., 1946-, photographer (tl); LC-DIG-ppmsca-39789 / Johnston, Frances Benjamin, 1864-1952, photographer (br). **14 Alamy Stock Photo:** Jonathan Ernst / UPI (cla). **15 Getty Images:** Corbis Historical / Leif Skoogfors (bl). **16 Getty Images:** Jabin Botsford / Pool (cl). **18 United States Senate:** U.S. Senate Collection (cl). **19 Getty Images:** Erin Schaff / The New York Times / Bloomberg (tr). **20 Alamy Stock Photo:** Everett Collection Inc (cra). **Getty Images:** Diana Walker / Liaison / Hulton Archive (bl). **21 Alamy Stock Photo:** Ron Sachs / CNP / ZUMA Press, Inc. (br). **22 Alamy Stock Photo:** White House Photo (cra). Getty Images: Mandel Ngan / AFP (bl). **23 Getty Images:** Mark Wilson / Staff (cra). **24 Alamy Stock Photo:** Everett Collection Historical (bl). **Dreamstime.com:** Petr Svec (cl). **25 Getty Images:** AFP / Luke Frazza / Staff (cr). **26 Alamy Stock Photo:** PF-(usna) (cra). **29 Alamy Stock Photo:** Mark Reinstein / MediaPunch Inc (tr). Getty Images: Gado / Archive Photos (bl). **30 Alamy Stock Photo:** Globe Photos / ZUMA Press, Inc. (cl). **31 Alamy Stock Photo:** Niday Picture Library (bl). **Dreamstime.com:** Palinchak (cr). **32 Alamy Stock Photo:** Planetpix / DOD Photo (cra). **Getty Images:** Bill Pugliano / Stringer (bl). **33 Alamy Stock Photo:** Shawshots (tr). **Getty Images:** Bettmann (bc). **34 Getty Images / iStock:** E+ / JohnnyGreig (cla). **35 Getty Images:** Drew Angerer / Staff (br). **36 Collection of the Supreme Court of the United States:** (cra). **The US National Archives and Records Administration:** National Archives photo no. 210-CT-23-T380 (bl). **37 Getty Images:** Heritage Images / Hulton Fine Art Collection (cra). **38 Alamy Stock Photo:** Olivier Douliery / Abaca Press (cla). **42 Shutterstock.com:** EQRoy (cr). **43 Alamy Stock Photo:** Bob Daemmrich (tr). **44 Getty Images:** AFP / Saul Loeb / Staff (cla). **45 Alamy Stock Photo:** Ron Sachs / CNP / dpa picture alliance (cra). **47 Alamy Stock Photo:** Photo Researchers / Science History Images (cr). **Getty Images:** AFP / Saul Loeb / Staff (br); Chip Somodevilla / Staff (tr).

All other images © Dorling Kindersley Limited

Illustrations by: Karen Saavedra

For the curious
www.dk.com

CONTENTS

WELCOMING THE
PRESIDENT

★ ★

Every four years on January 20, tens of thousands of Americans gather in the nation's capital, Washington, D.C. They come to see an **inauguration–the ceremony that marks the start of a U.S. president's time in office**. The president serves as head of the national, or federal, government. At the inauguration, the president promises to defend the Constitution, the document which created that federal government in 1787.

Governments create and enforce laws to meet the needs of their citizens, keeping people safe and helping them when they need it. Some governments are led by a king or queen. Others are ruled by members of the military. **The United States is a republic.**

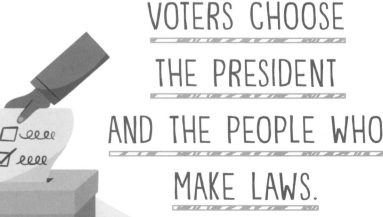

VOTERS CHOOSE THE PRESIDENT AND THE PEOPLE WHO MAKE LAWS.

★ WHAT IS A ★ REPUBLIC?

- In a republic, **the voters** are the true source of the government's power.

- The people elected make and carry out laws based on the voters' needs and wants.

- If voters don't like what these representatives do, **they can vote** for someone else in the next election.

OTHER GOVERNMENTS

The federal government shares its powers with the **50 states**. Each of them has their own government, too. And, within the states, cities, towns, and counties also have local governments.

★ BY THE NUMBERS

The federal government includes people who aren't elected. More than two million workers help government officials do their jobs. Another **1.4 million** people belong to different branches of the U.S. military.

CREATING THE
U.S. GOVERNMENT

★ ★

On May 25, 1787, 55 men met in Philadelphia, Pennsylvania, to create a new government for the United States. **Delegates**, or representatives from all of the 13 states that existed at the time, except Rhode Island, attended. They chose George Washington to lead what is now called the **Constitutional Convention**.

GEORGE WASHINGTON

The U.S. became an independent nation in 1783. Before the Constitutional Convention, the country's national government did not have much power. Some American leaders wanted a stronger national government. Through a long, hot summer, the delegates debated what powers the U.S. government should have.

Finally, they decided the government would be divided into three branches, or parts: Congress would make laws, the president would enforce them, and courts would settle arguments over federal laws. The three branches would share power so that one branch did not control the government. This idea is called **separation of powers**. The federal government would also share some powers with the states.

★ WHAT IS A ★
CONSTITUTION?

A constitution is a set of rules about how the government of a country works. Constitutions often have three main parts:

- the system of government, such as a federal system with a central government and individual state governments

- what the government does and how laws are made

- the rights of citizens.

MEMBERS OF CONGRESS SWEAR THAT THEY WILL UPHOLD THE CONSTITUTION.

THIS IS A PAINTING OF THE CONSTITUTIONAL CONVENTION. HOW DO YOU THINK THIS PICTURE WOULD BE DIFFERENT IF IT SHOWED MEMBERS OF THE U.S. CONGRESS TODAY? THE CLOTHES PEOPLE ARE WEARING WOULD CERTAINLY HAVE CHANGED. BUT WHAT ABOUT THE PEOPLE THEMSELVES?

On September 17, 1787, the delegates approved the Constitution of the United States. The next year, 9 of the 13 states approved the Constitution, too. The United States had a new government.

CHANGING THE CONSTITUTION

★ ★ ★ ★ ★ ★ ★ ★ ★ ★ ★ ★ ★ ★ ★ ★ ★ ★ ★

Some Americans thought the Constitution didn't do enough to protect their rights. When Congress first met in 1789, James Madison of Virginia proposed adding **12 amendments**, or changes, to the Constitution. By 1791, the country had approved ten of these changes. These amendments are called the Bill of Rights.

The amendments said that the government could not deny freedom of speech or the freedom of the press. People could also follow any religion they chose. The Bill of Rights also said people charged with a crime should get a speedy trial.

The **Bill of Rights** did not protect all Americans. Enslaved people and Indigenous people, amongst others, were not given the same rights. But today, all Americans should have the rights listed in the Bill of Rights and the rest of the Constitution.

INDIGENOUS AMERICANS WERE NOT SEEN AS FULL CITIZENS AT THE TIME OF THE BILL OF RIGHTS.

THE AMENDMENT PROCESS

The delegates at the Constitutional Convention did not want to make it too easy to change the government.

TO MAKE ANY CHANGES TO THE CONSTITUTION, THREE QUARTERS OF THE STATES MUST RATIFY, OR APPROVE, THEM.

★ BILL OF RIGHTS ★

Since the Bill of Rights was approved, Congress has considered more than 11,000 amendments. Only 37 of them have gone to the states for them to consider.

> THE BILL OF RIGHTS GUARANTEED FREEDOM OF RELIGION TO ALL AMERICANS.

A Bill of Rights
as provided in the Ten Original Amendments to
The Constitution of the United States
in force December 15, 1791.

Article I

Congress shall make no law respecting an establishment of religion, or prohibiting the free exercise thereof; or abridging the freedom of speech, or of the press; or the right of the people peaceably to assemble, and to petition the Government for a redress of grievances.

Article II

A well regulated Militia, being necessary to the security of a free State, the right of the people to bear Arms, shall not be infringed.

or property, without due process of law; nor shall private property be taken for public use, without just compensation.

Article VI

In all criminal prosecutions, the accused shall enjoy the right to a speedy and public trial, by an impartial jury of the State and district wherein the crime shall have been committed, which district shall have been previously ascertained by law, and to be informed of the nature and cause of the accusation; to be confronted with the witnesses against him; to have compulsory process for obtaining Witnesses in his favor, and to have the Assistance of

A CHANGING DEMOCRACY

★ ★ ★ ★ ★ ★ ★ ★ ★ ★ ★ ★ ★ ★ ★ ★ ★ ★

As the U.S. grew, many Americans demanded more rights. This led to more changes to the Constitution. Since 1791, Congress and the states have ratified 17 more amendments. Here are some of the most important ones.

★ THIRTEENTH AMENDMENT, 1865

The Civil War (1861–1865) started because of slavery. Under slavery, one person treats another person as a piece of property and has total control over their life. After the war, this amendment made owning people as property illegal in all states.

★ FOURTEENTH AMENDMENT, 1868

Before this amendment, the protections in the Bill of Rights only applied to laws passed by the federal government. Some states did not want to grant formerly enslaved people their rights. This amendment made it clear that anyone born in the U.S. was both a U.S. citizen and a citizen of their state. States could not deny their citizens the rights protected by the Constitution.

★ FIFTEENTH AMENDMENT, 1870

This amendment gave Black men the right to vote. Some states, though, passed laws that made it almost impossible for them to use that right. A federal law passed in 1965 protected equal voting rights.

★ SIXTEENTH AMENDMENT, 1913

This amendment let Congress collect taxes on the money people earned. This makes it easier for the government to raise large amounts of money.

★ NINETEENTH AMENDMENT, 1920

From the late 19th century, some states gave women the right to vote. Many Americans campaigned for women in every state to have that right. This amendment gave women their voting rights.

★ TWENTY-SECOND AMENDMENT, 1951

The Constitution did not limit how long a president could serve. Most presidents did not run again after being elected twice. Franklin Roosevelt, though, ran and won four times. This amendment said a person could only be elected president twice.

★ TWENTY-SIXTH AMENDMENT, 1971

During the late 1960s, America was fighting a war in Vietnam. Many of the soldiers were not old enough to vote, and many Americans thought that was unfair. This amendment lowered the voting age to 18 for both federal and state elections.

WHAT HAPPENS IN CONGRESS?

★ ★

Inside the U.S. Capitol in Washington, D.C., Americans can watch their representatives debate what laws the country should have. The Capitol is the home of Congress, the **legislative**, or law-making, branch of the federal government.

★ TWO HOUSES IN ONE ★

Congress is divided into two parts, called **houses**. One is the House of Representatives, and the other is the Senate. The first Congress met in 1789 in New York City, which was then the nation's capital.

To pass a law, a majority of members in each house must vote in favor of it. Half of the members plus one equals a majority.

MANY WORDS DESCRIBING THE U.S. GOVERNMENT ARE TAKEN FROM ANCIENT ROME. IT ONCE HAD A REPUBLICAN GOVERNMENT, TOO, WHICH INCLUDED A BODY CALLED THE SENATE. THE ROMANS SPOKE LATIN, AND LEGISLATIVE COMES FROM THE LATIN WORD LEGIS, WHICH MEANS "LAW".

CHECKS AND BALANCES

Along with the idea of separation of powers, the Constitution was designed to include checks and balances. This means that one government branch often has to work with another to get something done. For example, **Congress** doesn't act alone in making laws—the president usually must approve them, too. The checks and balances are another way to make sure one branch of the government does not have too much power over the other branches.

CHECKS AND BALANCES ARE AT WORK WITHIN CONGRESS, TOO.

The **delegates** at the Constitutional Convention wanted to balance the power of the large and small states. So, the number of members of the House of Representatives is based on each state's population. That gives more representatives to states with more people, such as California. But each state has only two senators, which gives smaller states an equal voice in the Senate.

THE HOUSE OF REPRESENTATIVES

★ ★ ★ ★ ★ ★ ★ ★ ★ ★ ★ ★ ★ ★ ★ ★ ★ ★ ★ ★

On January 4, 2007, Nancy Pelosi of California made history. She became the first woman to serve as Speaker of the House, the most important position in the House of Representatives. Like all Speakers, Pelosi played a major part in deciding which bills, or proposed laws, the other representatives would debate.

Today, the House of Representatives has 435 members. Each member represents an area in their state called a Congressional district. On average, each district has about 750,000 people. Only people who have registered, or signed up, can vote to elect a representative. Each state has at least one representative, and a state can gain or lose seats in the House if its population goes up or down. The U.S. population is counted every ten years so that the number of representatives can be adjusted, if necessary. The count is called a **census**.

Once elected, a representative serves a two-year term. When that period ends, the representative can choose to run for election again or leave the House. If a representative dies or quits before the end of their term, voters choose a new representative in a special election.

JOHN DINGELL JR. OF MICHIGAN SERVED LONGER IN THE HOUSE THAN ANY OTHER REPRESENTATIVE—ALMOST 60 YEARS!

★ FIGHTING SHIRLEY ★

Shirley Chisholm of New York was the first Black woman elected to the House of Representatives. She served from 1969 to 1983. She earned the nickname "Fighting Shirley" because of her work to make sure people of color and women received equal rights. Chisholm was also the first Black American to try to run for president as a member of a major political party.

THE HOUSE
AT WORK

★ ★ ★ ★ ★ ★ ★ ★ ★ ★ ★ ★ ★ ★ ★ ★ ★ ★ ★ ★

The House of Representatives has several special duties, given to it by the Constitution. Only the House can propose bills that collect taxes. The House also can **impeach** the president and other federal officials, which means they can charge them with doing something wrong. That could lead to the officials being removed from office. The House can choose the president if there is no winner in an election.

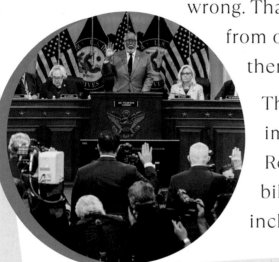

The Speaker of the House is the most important position in the House of Representatives. Along with deciding which bills will be debated, the Speaker's duties include:

- presiding over, or managing sessions in the House, which includes choosing who gets to speak

- enforcing House rules

- calling for votes

- leading other members of their party in the House.

If for some reason both the president and the vice president cannot serve, the Speaker steps in to serve as president. So far, this has never happened.

COMMITTEES

House members do a lot of their work in groups called **committees**. The leader of a committee is called the chair. The political party with a majority of members in the House gets to choose the chair. Each committee debates bills related to a topic, such as energy or the military.

DID YOU KNOW?

THE SPEAKER'S INFLUENCE CAN EVEN SHAPE THE MENU IN THE HOUSE DINING ROOM. IN 1904, SPEAKER JOSEPH CANNON ORDERED THAT BEAN SOUP, HIS FAVORITE SOUP, BE SERVED EVERY DAY. IT HAS BEEN SERVED EVER SINCE!

Committees also hold **hearings**—public meetings where people with special knowledge on a subject speak. After holding hearings, committee members can add amendments to a bill. Then they vote on whether the bill should go to the full House of Representatives for a vote.

THE SENATE

★ ★

Hiram Revels of Mississippi made history when he walked into the U.S. Senate chamber in 1870. **He became the first Black American senator.** Freed Black Americans from across the country turned to him for help. After Revels, Mississippi elected another Black American senator—Blanche K. Bruce in 1874. However, no other Black politician served there for almost 100 years. One reason was that many states passed laws that made it hard for Black Americans to vote.

BLANCHE K. BRUCE

The U.S. Senate has 100 members, with two from each state. That means that a state with around 600,000 people, such as Wyoming, has as much power in the Senate as California, which has 40 million people. People in quiet, rural areas will often have more influence in the Senate than people in busy cities, because, with fewer people around, each person's individual voice has a greater impact.

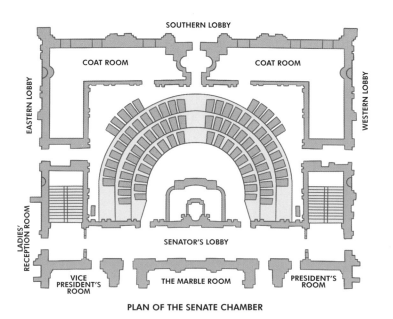

SOUTHERN LOBBY

COAT ROOM   COAT ROOM

EASTERN LOBBY   WESTERN LOBBY

LADIES' RECEPTION ROOM

SENATOR'S LOBBY

VICE PRESIDENT'S ROOM   THE MARBLE ROOM   PRESIDENT'S ROOM

PLAN OF THE SENATE CHAMBER

Senators serve six-year terms, but every seat is not up for election at the same time. Every two years, about one third of the senators' terms end. If a senator dies or leaves office before the end of their term, most state governors can name someone to complete the term. Some states, though, hold a special election to fill the empty seat.

THE SENATE ALSO HAS A PRESIDENT. THE VICE PRESIDENT OF THE COUNTRY FILLS THIS ROLE.

SENATE POWERS

The Constitution gives the **Senate** some special powers. When a president chooses federal judges and many other government officials, a majority of senators must approve the choice. The Senate must also approve any treaties that the president makes with foreign nations. Two thirds of the senators must vote for the treaty. If the House impeaches a federal official, the Senate then acts like a court. It decides if the impeached person should be removed from office.

DID YOU KNOW?

TO SERVE IN THE SENATE, A PERSON MUST:

• BE AT LEAST 30 YEARS OLD

• HAVE BEEN A U.S. CITIZEN FOR AT LEAST NINE YEARS

• BE A RESIDENT IN THE STATE THEY REPRESENT AT THE TIME OF THEIR ELECTION.

THE SENATE AT
WORK

★ ★ ★ ★ ★ ★ ★ ★ ★ ★ ★ ★ ★ ★ ★ ★ ★ ★ ★ ★

The most powerful person in the Senate is the majority leader, who is chosen by the political party with the most seats. Like the Speaker of the House, the majority leader decides which bills the Senate will debate.

As in the House, most of the important work on bills is done by committees. The majority party gets to pick the chairs of the committees.

MIKE MANSFIELD IS THE LONGEST-SERVING MAJORITY LEADER IN THE HISTORY OF THE SENATE. HE SERVED 16 YEARS, FROM 1961 UNTIL HIS RETIREMENT IN 1977.

★ THE FILIBUSTER ★

Senators use the filibuster to delay or prevent a vote on a bill. Senators might think that a bill is unfair to certain groups of Americans, and, using the filibuster, can stop the bill from being approved.

The Senate used to let members speak for as long as they could during a filibuster. However, 60 senators could vote to end it. That vote is called a **cloture**.

STROM THURMOND OF SOUTH CAROLINA SET THE RECORD FOR THE LONGEST FILIBUSTER. IN 1957, HE SPOKE WITHOUT STOPPING FOR 24 HOURS AND 18 MINUTES.

Today, senators just say that they want a filibuster, and there is no vote on it unless enough senators vote for a cloture. Some Americans would like to end the filibuster, since many bills now require 60 votes to pass, rather than just a majority. But some senators argue that the filibuster forces the majority party to write bills that the other party can support. This means that the finished bill will reflect the views of more voters.

★ WOMEN IN ★ THE SENATE

Japanese American Mazie Hirono made history in 2012. She was the first Asian American woman elected to the U.S. Senate. Born in Japan, she later moved to Hawaii. She represented voters there in both the House and the Senate. The number of female senators has grown over the past few decades, but they still make up only about one in four of the members.

THE PRESIDENT

★ ★

On January 20, 2009, Barack Obama became the 44th president of the United States. He was the first Black American president. That day, he told Americans that the country could solve the problems it faced. Americans look to their presidents to lead the country through difficult times.

The president is the head of the executive branch of the U.S. government. That branch executes, or carries out, the laws passed by Congress. Presidents can't do whatever they want, but they do have many powers. The powers described in the Constitution are called expressed powers. One of the most important is the power to consider bills passed by Congress. Presidents sign a bill if they want it to become law. If they don't sign the bill, that means they have vetoed, or rejected it. Congress, though, can override, or reject, the veto, if two thirds of the members in both the Senate and House want the bill.

Since George Washington first vetoed a bill in 1792, U.S. presidents have issued more than 2,500 vetoes.

SOME PRESIDENTS USE MANY PENS WHEN THEY SIGN AN IMPORTANT BILL INTO LAW—SOMETIMES ONE PEN FOR EACH LETTER OF THEIR NAME. THE PRESIDENTS THEN GIVE THE PENS TO LAWMAKERS OR OTHERS WHO HELPED GET THE BILL PASSED IN CONGRESS.

★ COMMANDER IN CHIEF ★

The president is also in charge of the U.S. military. In that role, the president is called the commander in chief. Presidents cannot declare war against a foreign nation. Only Congress can do that.

Other expressed powers are:

- choosing federal judges, and other officials, which the Senate must approve

- making treaties with foreign nations

- reporting on the state of the country

- proposing laws to Congress

- pardoning people who have committed a crime

- calling Congress to meet during an emergency.

Some presidential powers are not spelled out in the Constitution. These are called informal powers. One of these is giving executive orders. These orders direct how the executive branch should carry out laws or rulings made by federal courts.

DID YOU KNOW?

TO BECOME PRESIDENT, A PERSON MUST:

- BE AT LEAST 35 YEARS OLD

- BE A NATURAL-BORN CITIZEN— THEY WERE BORN IN THE U.S.

- HAVE LIVED IN THE U.S. FOR 14 YEARS.

IF YOU WERE ELECTED PRESIDENT, WHAT WOULD YOU DO TO MAKE THE COUNTRY BETTER?

A PRESIDENT'S LIFE

★ ★

★ THE WHITE HOUSE ★

In 1800, John Adams became the first U.S. president to live and work in the White House, in Washington, D.C. Today, the White House has 132 rooms and 35 bathrooms. Presidents can also enjoy the house's own tennis court, bowling alley, swimming pool, and movie theater.

Presidents earn $400,000 every year they are in office. They use some of that money to pay for food and other items used at the White House. Those items include toothpaste and toilet paper!

Two presidents chose to donate their salary to charity: Herbert Hoover and John F. Kennedy.

THIS IS THE PRESIDENT'S COUNTRY RESIDENCE IN MARYLAND, CAMP DAVID. IT HAS A SWIMMING POOL, BOWLING ALLEY, GOLF COURSE AND MORE.

ON THE MOVE

Presidents need to keep working when they travel on **Air Force One**, their official plane. The plane has an office and a conference room, a doctor's office, and a kitchen that can feed 100 people.

Presidents also have a special car nicknamed the Beast. Its windows can stop bullets. The Beast has its own plane that takes it wherever the president goes.

A WORLD LEADER

Presidents also represent the U.S. around the world. They meet with leaders of other countries to discuss their shared interests. The U.S. is one of the world's richest and most powerful countries. Presidents use that strength to defend the U.S. and its interests.

WHAT DO YOU THINK PRESIDENT BUSH WANTED AMERICANS TO THINK AFTER HEARING HIS SPEECH?

On September 11, 2001, terrorists attacked the U.S., killing almost 3,000 people. President George W. Bush spoke to the nation that evening. In part, he said:

"None of us will ever forget this day. Yet, we go forward to defend freedom and all that is good and just in our world."

HOW ARE LAWS MADE?

In 1965, President Lyndon B. Johnson signed a bill called the **Voting Rights Act**. It stopped states from forcing Black and Hispanic Americans to pay a tax or prove they could read before they could vote. Johnson's signature officially made the bill a federal law.

PRESIDENT LYNDON JOHNSON SIGNS THE VOTING RIGHTS ACT.

INTRODUCTION

The process of making a new law starts in either house of Congress. A representative or senator presents a bill for their whole house to consider. The idea may have come from the lawmaker, voters, businesses, or other groups. Presidents can also ask members of Congress to present bills that they want to become law.

★ COMMITTEE ★

When a bill is in committee, experts explain why a bill is good or bad. Members of the executive branch can speak, too. The hearings help lawmakers learn how a bill will affect Americans if it becomes law.

★ HOUSE VOTES ★

If it is approved by committee, all members of the House and Senate vote on it. In the House, the Speaker chooses which bills will be voted on. Members vote using an electronic system that records their votes. In the Senate, the majority leader decides which bills will be voted on. Senators vote by saying either yea (yes) or nay (no).

★ PRESIDENT ★

When a bill is approved in both houses, it goes to the president. The president has ten days, not counting Sundays, to sign the bill into law or veto it.

★ BILL BECOMES LAW ★

Once it is approved by the president, the bill becomes a law.

ELECTING
A PRESIDENT

★ ★

In the 2016 presidential race, almost 3 million more people voted for Hillary Clinton than her opponent Donald Trump. Even so, Trump was elected president. Unlike in a Congressional election, a person running for president can lose the **popular vote** and still win. That's because presidents are elected state by state in the **Electoral College**.

States that are home to lots of people, such as California and Texas, have more electoral votes. There are a total of 538 electoral votes. A **candidate** for president must win 270 electoral votes to be elected president. Normally, they do that by winning the popular votes in different states. The popular vote winner usually takes all of the state's electoral votes.

So, in Michigan, the candidate who receives the most votes, even if they only get one more than their opponent, wins Michigan's 16 electoral votes.

The leaders of the political parties in each state choose who will serve as presidential electors. In most states, only the party representing the winner of the popular vote has its electors vote in the Electoral College.

IF THERE IS A TIE VOTE IN THE ELECTORAL COLLEGE, THE HOUSE OF REPRESENTATIVES CHOOSES THE PRESIDENT. THIS HAS ONLY HAPPENED ONCE, IN 1824, WHEN JOHN QUINCY ADAMS WAS ELECTED.

DID YOU KNOW?

THESE PRESIDENTS LOST THE POPULAR VOTE BUT WERE STILL ELECTED:

JOHN QUINCY ADAMS, 1824

RUTHERFORD B. HAYES, 1876

BENJAMIN HARRISON, 1888

GEORGE W. BUSH, 2000

DONALD TRUMP, 2016

REMOVING
A PRESIDENT

★ ★ ★ ★ ★ ★ ★ ★ ★ ★ ★ ★ ★ ★ ★ ★ ★ ★ ★

In 1999, President Bill Clinton faced a trial in the Senate. He had been accused of breaking two laws. The Senate had to decide if he was guilty and should be removed from office. In the end, the Senate found Clinton not guilty.

Clinton's trial was part of a process called **impeachment**. It lets

Congress remove a federal official from office if he or she is accused of breaking the law. The accusations might include taking money illegally or betraying the country in some way. Officials can also be impeached for misusing their power.

Impeachment begins in the House of Representatives. A member can introduce a **resolution**, which is like a bill, except it only affects Congress. The resolution calls for the House to see if a government official should be impeached.

If the resolution passes, a House committee gathers evidence against the official accused of breaking the law. The committee then tells the entire House if they believe the person should be impeached. If the House votes to impeach, a trial begins in the Senate.

During this trial, members of the House act like lawyers. They present evidence against the accused person. The accused official also has lawyers who defend them. The senators are the **jury**. They decide if the person facing impeachment should be removed from office. If at least 67 senators find them guilty, the official must leave office.

PRESIDENTIAL IMPEACHMENT

Only three presidents have faced impeachment trials: Andrew Johnson in 1868, Bill Clinton, and Donald Trump, who was tried in 2019 and 2021. None of them were found guilty and so were not removed from office.

DONALD TRUMP

ONLY EIGHT PEOPLE, ALL OF THEM JUDGES, HAVE BEEN REMOVED FROM THEIR JOB AFTER A FEDERAL IMPEACHMENT TRIAL.

ANDREW JOHNSON

THE VICE PRESIDENT

★ ★ ★ ★ ★ ★ ★ ★ ★ ★ ★ ★ ★ ★ ★ ★ ★ ★ ★

When Joe Biden ran for president in 2020, he chose Kamala Harris as his **running mate**. That meant that when Biden won, Harris became the vice president. She was the first woman, first Black American and first Asian American to hold that important position.

If a president dies, quits, or is too sick to serve, the vice president takes over. The Constitution does not say much else about the vice president's role, other than serving as president of the Senate. In that role, the vice president votes to break any ties. The vice president also announces the name of the person elected president after the counting of the electoral votes.

VICE PRESIDENT KAMALA HARRIS

In recent years, presidents have relied on vice presidents to give them **advice**. Some presidents also ask their vice president to study problems the country faces. For example, Biden asked Harris to study why people choose to leave their own countries to come to the U.S.

If a vice president dies or leaves office, the president chooses a new one. Each house of Congress, though, must approve this choice.

SERVING UNDER GEORGE W. BUSH, DICK CHENEY WAS ONE OF THE MOST POWERFUL VICE PRESIDENTS EVER.

JOHN ADAMS

OPPOSING ★ PARTIES ★

In the first three presidential elections, the person who came in second in the Electoral College vote became vice president. That person and the president could belong to different parties, which could lead to disagreements. This happened when John Adams was elected president in 1796, and Thomas Jefferson was elected vice president.

HARRY S. TRUMAN BECAME PRESIDENT AFTER THE DEATH OF FRANKLIN ROOSEVELT IN 1944.

THE EXECUTIVE BRANCH

★ ★

The president is sometimes called the chief executive, because they are in charge of the executive branch. This branch of government is made up of different parts called departments. Each department carries out laws related to a specific area of government. Their actions affect many parts of your life. For example, money from some departments helps states and towns build roads and pay for police. Other executive branch programs help farmers put food on your table.

The U.S. government currently has 15 departments. Department leaders are chosen by the president, with the Senate's approval. All but one of these leaders is called a secretary. The head of the Justice Department is called the attorney general.

The heads of the executive departments give advice to the president. Together, they form the presidential **cabinet**. Presidents may also ask other officials to serve in their cabinet, such as the vice president and the heads of smaller, but important, agencies.

THE DEPARTMENT OF EDUCATION IS IN CHARGE OF AMERICA'S SCHOOLS.

THE EXECUTIVE DEPARTMENTS

Agriculture
Commerce
Defense
Education

Energy
Health and Human Services
Homeland Security

Housing and Urban Development
Interior
Justice

Labor
State
Transportation
Treasury
Veterans Affairs

CABINET STARS

Some cabinet members have made their mark on U.S. history:

In 1933, **Frances Perkins** became the first woman to lead an executive department. As secretary of Labor, she helped create Social Security. This government program ensures people will have money after they are too old or sick to work.

Robert Weaver became secretary of Housing and Urban Development (HUD) in 1966. He was the first Black American to serve in a presidential cabinet. At HUD, he supported a law that tried to improve housing in cities.

The Interior Department plays a large role in helping Indigenous nations. In 2021, **Deb Haaland** became the first Indigenous person to lead that or any other executive department. One of her goals was to improve the lives of Indigenous people by reducing crime on tribal lands.

DEB HAALAND

THE SUPREME COURT

★ ★ ★ ★ ★ ★ ★ ★ ★ ★ ★ ★ ★ ★ ★ ★ ★ ★ ★ ★

The third branch of the U.S. government is the **judicial** branch. This is a system of federal courts. The most powerful one is the Supreme Court. Its decisions have deeply shaped U.S. history. These include striking down laws that denied people of color and LGBTQ+ people their rights.

> IN 2022, KETANJI BROWN JACKSON BECAME THE FIRST BLACK WOMAN TO SERVE ON THE SUPREME COURT.

> MITSUYE ENDO WON THE SUPREME COURT CASE THAT SAID THE GOVERNMENT COULD NOT PUT LOYAL U.S. CITIZENS IN PRISON.

During World War II, about 120,000 Japanese Americans were taken from their homes and held prisoner by the U.S. government. Most were U.S. citizens. The U.S. government feared they might try to help Japan defeat the U.S. After several legal battles, the U.S. Supreme Court ruled that loyal U.S. citizens held prisoner should be released. The **Court** found that the executive branch did not have the power to detain those Americans.

THE COURT AND ITS MEMBERS

The Supreme Court has nine judges, called **justices**. The Constitution does not say how many justices there should be, so the number can change. The head of the Court is called the Chief Justice. All justices are chosen by the president, though the Senate must approve these choices. Once on the Court, justices can serve for life, or until they choose to retire, unless they are impeached.

The Supreme Court mostly hears cases that begin in lower federal courts (see page 38). The loser of a case can file an appeal. This means they want the **Supreme Court** to decide if the lower courts ruled correctly. The Supreme Court usually hears cases to decide if federal or some state laws are allowed under the Constitution. If the Court decides a law is not allowed, it is no longer enforced.

JOHN MARHSALL REMAINS THE LONGEST-SERVING CHIEF JUSTICE AND FOURTH-LONGEST SERVING JUSTICE IN THE HISTORY OF THE U.S. SUPREME COURT.

OTHER FEDERAL
COURTS

★ ★ ★ ★ ★ ★ ★ ★ ★ ★ ★ ★ ★ ★ ★ ★ ★ ★ ★ ★

Federal district and appeals courts are part of the judicial branch of government. Like all courts, they decide if someone has broken a law. Everyone has to follow the same laws, including governments. Governments sometimes break the law just as ordinary people do.

In 1992, President George H.W. Bush nominated Sonia Sotomayor to be a judge on a federal district court. Sotomayor heard about 450 cases there, before moving on to a U.S. appeals court. In 2009, she joined the U.S. Supreme Court, making her the first Hispanic justice.

Cases that involve federal laws are first heard in one of the country's 94 district courts. Each of these courts has one or more judges, chosen by the president, that the Senate must **confirm**. Like Supreme Court justices, these judges can serve for life.

ALL BUT ONE OF THE DISTRICT COURTS
ALSO HAS A DISTRICT ATTORNEY.

District attorneys and their staff collect and present evidence against someone accused of a crime. District attorneys are also chosen by the president and serve four-year terms. A president may ask a district attorney to serve longer.

COURT OF APPEALS

The United States has 13 courts of appeals, which are also called circuit courts. If someone loses a case in a district court, they can appeal it to one of these courts to see if the district court made the correct decision. The number of judges on a circuit court ranges from 6 to 29. These judges are also chosen by the president and confirmed by the Senate. In most cases, just three of the judges on a court hear an appeal.

Law cases are either **criminal** or **civil**. A criminal case means someone is accused of breaking the law. A civil case involves a dispute between two or more people or groups. Federal courts hear both kinds of cases.

POLITICAL PARTIES

When people register to vote, they can choose to join a **political party**. A party is a group of voters and government officials who share similar views on what laws should be passed and how the country should be run.

TODAY, THE UNITED STATES HAS TWO MAJOR POLITICAL PARTIES.

THE REPUBLICAN PARTY FORMED IN 1854. IN GENERAL, THE PARTY:

- SEEKS TO LIMIT THE POWER OF THE FEDERAL GOVERNMENT OVER THE STATES

- TRIES TO KEEP TAXES LOW

- OPPOSES LAWS THAT LIMIT WHAT BUSINESSES CAN DO TO MAKE MONEY.

THE DEMOCRATIC PARTY FORMED AROUND 1830. IN GENERAL, THE PARTY:

- BELIEVES THE FEDERAL GOVERNMENT SHOULD USE ITS POWER TO HELP AS MANY PEOPLE AS POSSIBLE

- PROTECTS THE RIGHTS OF WOMEN, PEOPLE OF COLOR AND LGBTQ+ AMERICANS

- WANTS THE FEDERAL GOVERNMENT TO PROTECT THE ENVIRONMENT.

ALEXANDER HAMILTON AND THOMAS JEFFERSON
LED THE FIRST U.S. POLITICAL PARTIES.

The Constitution does not mention political parties. They developed on their own soon after George Washington was elected president in 1789. At the time, people debated what kind of government the country should have. Some Americans favored a strong federal government and wanted to promote business and trade. Others wanted to limit the power of the federal government and favored the interests of farmers.

✦ SMALLER PARTIES ✦

The United States also has smaller parties called third parties. They might focus on a specific issue. Not all third parties are active in every state. The Libertarian Party is the largest of these parties. Since 1972, the Libertarians have always had a candidate for president.

AMERICAN VOTERS DO NOT HAVE TO CHOOSE TO JOIN A PARTY. THEY CAN REGISTER AS AN INDEPENDENT.

CAMPAIGNS

★ ★ ★ ★ ★ ★ ★ ★ ★ ★ ★ ★ ★ ★ ★ ★ ★ ★ ★ ★

To become president or a member of Congress, people first have to convince their own party that they can do the job. Then they try to convince all voters of the same thing. **The effort to win an election is called a campaign.**

Candidates start their campaigns by hiring people to work for them. That means they must raise money to pay them. The money comes from voters, businesses, and groups who support the candidate's views.

Political parties also spend money to help their candidates. Some of this money is used to buy advertisements that appear in social media, on television, or in newspapers.

The amount of money needed to win a political race concerns some people. They fear elected officials will mostly help the people who give them the most money. Another concern is that candidates with the most money have a better chance of winning.

★ PRIMARIES ★

If more than one member of a party wants the same seat, they face each other in an election called a **primary**. Primaries are held every four years to choose a candidate for president. The party's candidates travel across the country to try to win as many votes in each state as possible. The voters are choosing delegates for their party. The delegates will vote for the person they support at a party meeting called a convention. The winning presidential candidate then chooses their running mate. These two people will run against the other party's choice for president and vice president.

DID YOU KNOW?

SOME STATES CHOOSE PRESIDENTIAL CANDIDATES AT A MEETING CALLED A CAUCUS. THESE ARE RUN BY THE POLITICAL PARTIES. MEMBERS OF A PARTY TRY TO CONVINCE THEIR FRIENDS AND NEIGHBORS TO SUPPORT THE CANDIDATE THEY LIKE.

ELECTION DAY

★ ★ ★ ★ ★ ★ ★ ★ ★ ★ ★ ★ ★ ★ ★ ★ ★ ★ ★ ★

Every two years, usually on the first Tuesday in November, millions of Americans head to the polls—the places where elections are held. These voters choose who will serve their interests in government.

In federal elections, voters choose who will represent them in Congress. Every four years, voters also elect a president. Elections for state and local leaders are often held on the same day as the federal election.

VOTERS USUALLY MARK WHICH CANDIDATES THEY PREFER ON PIECES OF PAPER CALLED BALLOTS.

In some states, they might use a machine instead. Candidates and voters often know who has won a race by the end of Election Day, unless the race is close. Then it might take time to name a winner. In very close races, state law might call for the votes to be counted again. Candidates in close races can also call for a recount.

AFTER THE ★ ELECTION ★

In the January following the elections, new members of Congress are sworn in. This means they promise to defend the Constitution of the United States. Presidents do the same thing during their inauguration. Then, the lawmakers and the president begin their jobs of creating and enforcing laws. Their actions shape your life. When you're old enough to vote, you will help decide who carries out these important jobs. What do you think makes a good political candidate?

DID YOU KNOW?

NOT ALL VOTERS GO TO THE POLLS ON ELECTION DAY. SOME STATES ALLOW THEM TO VOTE BY:

- MAILING IN BALLOTS BEFORE ELECTION DAY

- DROPPING OFF BALLOTS AT SPECIAL BOXES IN OR OUTSIDE PUBLIC BUILDINGS

- VOTING EARLY IN PERSON

EIGHT STATES DO ALL THEIR VOTING BY MAIL.

GLOSSARY

amendments
changes or additions to a legal document, such as a constitution

appeal
a legal request for one court to review a lower court's decision

bills
proposed laws debated in Congress

cabinet
the heads of executive agencies who advise a president and carry out their plans

candidate
a person running for a political office

census
a count of population done every ten years

cloture
a vote in the Senate to end debate on a bill

committees
small groups of lawmakers who review bills

confirm
approve a president's choice for government positions

Constitutional Convention
the meeting held in 1787 to create a new U.S. government

district
a geographic area represented by an elected lawmaker

Electoral College
the process by which the country elects its president

executive
referring to the branch of government that carries out and enforces laws

expressed powers
powers spelled out in the Constitution

federal
the name for the U.S. national government or any government with powers shared between states and a national government

filibuster
the process in the U.S. Senate for delaying a vote on a bill

inauguration
the swearing in of a new president

judicial
referring to the court system in a government

legislative
referring to the lawmaking body of a government

popular vote
the count of all the votes cast in a presidential election

primary
elections held by political parties to choose candidates

ratify
approve a treaty or legal document so that it takes effect

resolution
an act of Congress addressing emergencies or the rules of Congress

running mate
a presidential candidate's choice for vice president

separation of powers
the sharing of government powers between different branches

term
the length of time an elected official holds their job for

vetoed
stopped a bill from becoming a law

INDEX